LIFE IN THE ROMAN EMPIRE

# THE COUNTRYSIDE
# IN THE
# ROMAN EMPIRE

ALLISON LANE

Cavendish
Square
New York

Published in 2017 by Cavendish Square Publishing, LLC
243 5th Avenue, Suite 136, New York, NY 10016

Website: cavendishsq.com

This publication represents the opinions and views of the author based on his or her personal experience, knowledge, and research. The information in this book serves as a general guide only. The author and publisher have used their best efforts in preparing this book and disclaim liability rising directly or indirectly from the use and application of this book.

CPSIA Compliance Information: Batch #CW17CSQ

All websites were available and accurate when this book was sent to press.

Library of Congress Cataloging-in-Publication Data

Names: Lane, Allison, 1981- author.
Title: The countryside in the Roman Empire / Allison Lane.
Description: New York : Cavendish Square Publishing, [2017] |
Series: Life in the Roman Empire | Includes bibliographical references and index.
Identifiers: LCCN 2016026010 (print) | LCCN 2016033446 (ebook) |
ISBN 9781502622617 (library bound) | ISBN 9781502622624 (ebook)
Subjects: LCSH: Country life--Rome--History--Juvenile literature. |
Rome--Social life and customs--Juvenile literature. | Rome--Rural conditions--Juvenile literature. |
Rome--History--Empire, 30 B.C.-476 A.D.--Juvenile literature.
Classification: LCC DG78 .L36 2017 (print) | LCC DG78 (ebook) |
DDC 937/.06--dc23
LC record available at https://lccn.loc.gov/2016026010

Editorial Director: David McNamara
Editor: Caitlyn Miller
Copy Editor: Nathan Heidelberger
Associate Art Director: Amy Greenan
Designer: Joseph Macri
Production Coordinator: Karol Szymczuk
Photo Research: J8 Media

Printed in the United States of America

# Contents

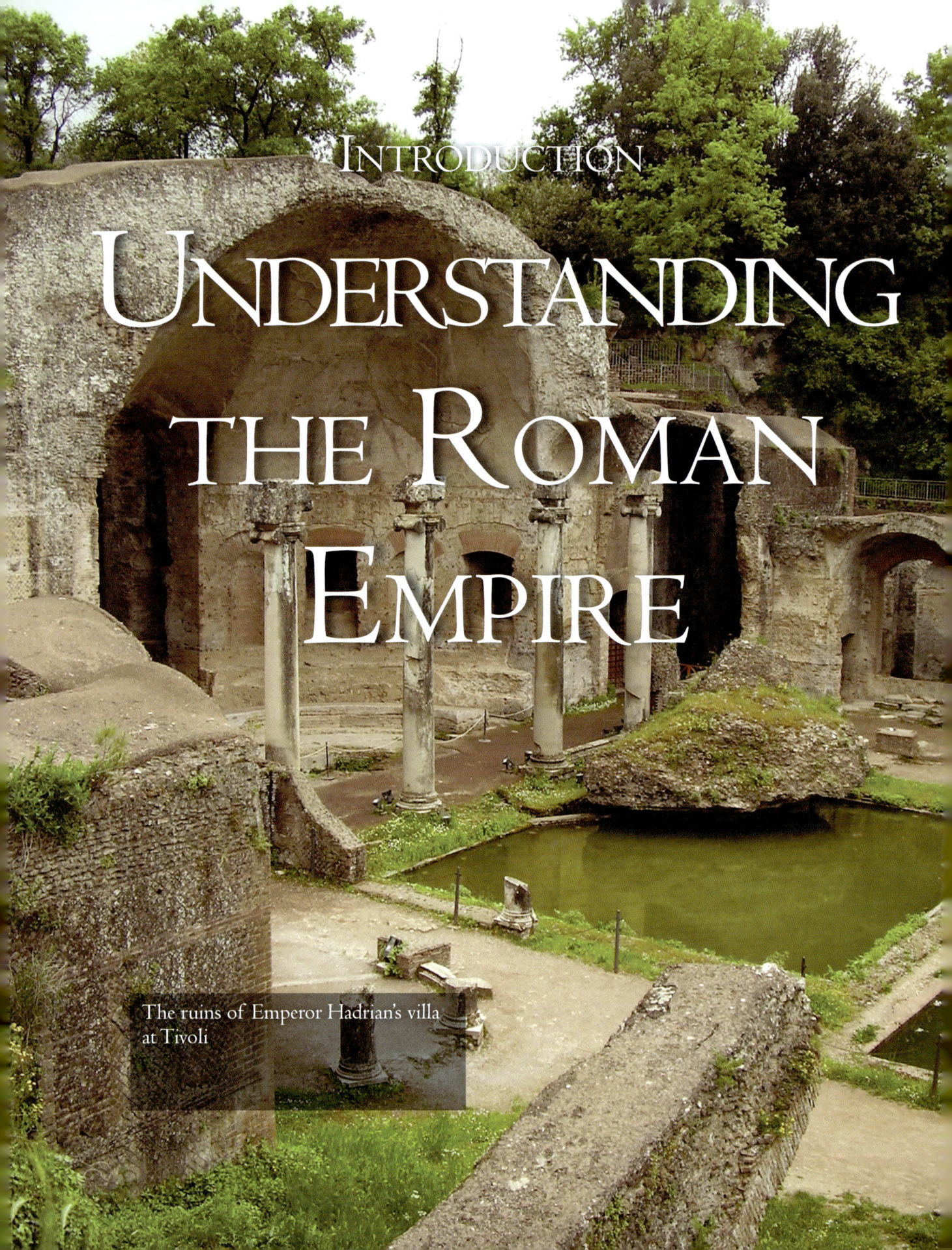

# UNDERSTANDING THE ROMAN EMPIRE

The ruins of Emperor Hadrian's villa at Tivoli

The history of the Roman Empire begins in 753 BCE with the establishment of the city of Rome. From there, rulers expanded the empire steadily. Augustus alone doubled the size of the empire during his rule. At its height, ancient Rome reached all the way from Britain to Persia.

The empire developed in other ways, too. While Rome began as a kingdom, it later transitioned to a republic. After the assassination of Julius Caesar, Rome would be ruled by emperors until the empire's end. Nero, Caligula, Hadrian, and Marcus Aurelius are just a few of the emperors whose power was so great that their names are recognized to this day.

Ancient Rome is famous for its powerful leaders, talented artists, and philosophers with big ideas. Its impact can be seen in our modern lives in everything from styles of architecture to styles of government. Works by Roman poets like Ovid and Virgil survive today and continue to be celebrated.

The Roman Empire has become synonymous with life in the great city itself and in all the other cities of the empire. Roman civilization was focused on urban life—even the word "civilization" comes from one of the Romans' words for "city," *civis*. Most people in the Roman Empire, however, did not live in cities. They lived in rural areas: on scattered farmsteads, in villages and small towns, or on plantation-like farming estates. Although history has largely ignored these people, their work as farmers, herders, spinners, and weavers—among other rural occupations—was critical to the strength and well-being of the Roman Empire. In this book you will meet farmers, slaves, soldiers, poets, and others who lived and worked in the rural areas ruled by Rome during the height of the empire (27 BCE to around 200 CE). Understanding these people is essential to the understanding of life in the Roman Empire.

# Chapter One

# The Backbone of the Empire

Farmers' tasks have been immortalized in funerary sculptures; this sarcophagus shows farmers raising crops and milking livestock.

> *"Planting is a thing not to be thought about but done."*
> —Cato

It's hard to imagine, but the population of ancient Rome was overwhelmingly rural. The Romans who lived in the countryside led lives that were very different from their urban counterparts. City dwellers relied on these people to grow the food that sustained the empire. Rural land provided strategic military outposts and even vacation spots for the wealthy. The well-being of the empire rested in the hands of farmers, whose work was idealized in poems like Virgil's *Georgics*. Yet country life was far from easy. Rural Romans toiled in the fields, tended to their livestock, and lived at the mercy of the seasons.

## A RURAL TRADITION

According to legend, the founder of Rome was Romulus, a shepherd. Many of his followers were shepherds, too, and farmers. The early city, in fact, was a union of farming villages scattered over seven neighboring hills. Even

The poet Virgil

after Rome was well on its way to becoming the greatest city on the Italian peninsula, the Romans thought of themselves as a nation of simple, honest, hard-working farmers. After Augustus came to power and Rome dominated the Mediterranean world, Romans still looked back with pride on their roots.

The countryside and rural life were celebrated not only by Virgil but by many other poets, including Horace, Tibullus, and Martial. The authors Varro and Columella composed treatises on agriculture. Author-statesman Pliny the Younger often wrote about his enjoyment of his country **villas** and his concerns about his farming estates. The historian Tacitus was one of many Romans who felt that society had become too "citified"—overly sophisticated, even decadent—and looked back on the "good old days" of the rural past. Horace, for example, says this about the great Romans of former times:

Those were the sons of farmers and soldiers too—tough males, accustomed, **mattock** in hand, to break hard clods, and bring home logs for firing under the eye of a mother stern and strong-willed.

Such authors—nearly all wealthy men who lived, at least part time, in the city—idealized country life. Unfortunately, we have very little written material from the common people whose lives centered on farming and other rural work. Few of these people knew how to read and write, and most of them worked too long and hard to take time for recording their experiences. Once in a while, though, we do hear the voice of someone from the countryside, as in this **inscription** from the tombstone of a North African man:

> From the day of my birth I have lived by working my land; neither my land nor I has ever had a rest … Twelve years' harvests I cut under the raging sun … and for eleven years I commanded teams of harvesters … Hard work, and contentment with little, finally brought me a home with a farmstead, and my home lacks nothing in wealth. Furthermore, my career has achieved the rewards of office … From a poor farm boy I actually became a censor [an official in the local government]. I have seen my children and my grandchildren grow up around me, and I have enjoyed years distinguished by the merits of my career … Thus has he deserved to die who has lived honourably.

## Sustenance and Support

In the ancient world, the country and cities generally had a very close relationship. Most cities controlled outlying rural areas, which depended on the cities for protection and supplied them with grain, vegetables, honey, wool, and other agricultural products. Usually there were many people who lived in cities but left them each day to work in the nearby fields. In numerous cases, there were fields, orchards, and pastures even within city walls.

Rome itself, with more than a million people, was so large that the surrounding region could not support it alone. More than six million sacks of grain a year were required to feed the city's residents. This grain was grown mainly in Sicily, Egypt, and other parts of North Africa. North Africa was also home to extensive olive orchards, as was Spain. Rome imported olive oil from both regions to meet the needs of its population. The oil was used in everything from cooking and lamp fuel to soaps and body lotions. Wine was another item exported from Spain to Rome in great quantity. Some of the best wines enjoyed by upper-class Romans, however, were produced in the vineyards scattered over the Italian countryside. Most of the pork and wool used in Rome came from the **province** of Cisalpine Gaul, the region of Italy just south of the Alps.

All over the empire, products flowed into cities from rural areas. The countryside provided a wide array of goods, from meat and milk, to linen and dyestuffs, to precious metals and building materials. Numerous cities, especially in the eastern empire, were as dependent on imported grain as Rome was. In many of these places, the surrounding region easily could have produced grain—but instead the land was used for the more profitable crops of grapes and olives. Basic food supplies often had to travel a long distance from country to city.

Another way in which the countryside played a supporting role to cities was by providing a place where busy urbanites could relax and "get away from it all" for a time. Rome (like other Mediterranean cities) was not only noisy and bustling, but in the summer it could be unbearably hot, so wealthy people migrated to villas in the hills or near the sea. Many villas were not simply "vacation homes" for their owners but were part of working farms. Agricultural products and the money from their sale were, in fact, the main source of wealth for many upper-class Romans.

## Fresh Food

Despite the fact that many rural Romans worked punishing jobs in the fields, there was one major benefit to living in the countryside: the food. Urban Romans relied on preserved fish, meat, and vegetables shipped from farms. Processes like salting and pickling kept food safe during the journey. (Scholars aren't sure if meats were smoked—it seems like they might have been.) On the other hand, those living in the country had access to fresh foods, including eggs, which were a common staple. Another big difference between urban and rural workers was the importance of lunch. People living in cities had a light lunch, but in the country it was often more involved to give workers the energy they needed to farm. Of course, diet varied in the countryside according to social class. Landowners who grew grapes and made wine often kept a share of their output. Alternatively, lower classes had more limited access to good food.

## REMOTE OUTPOSTS

Rome was the mightiest military power in the Western world. Its conquests gave it control over numerous diverse areas. Some parts of the empire were thickly urbanized, such as Italy, Greece, southern Spain, and the coasts of Asia Minor. Other provinces were far more rural, particularly in the north and west, with cities fewer and farther between. It was in these less urbanized areas, generally speaking, that the bulk of Rome's troops were stationed.

The remains of a Roman fortress in what is now Libya

The Roman army had two main divisions: the **legions** and the auxiliaries. Legionary soldiers were all Roman citizens, mostly from Italy and what are now Spain, southern France, and Turkey. The auxiliaries were soldiers recruited from the provinces. Some were citizens, but most earned Roman citizenship at the completion of their military service. The majority of legionnaires were foot soldiers, while auxiliaries often had specialized skills, such as fighting on horseback or using bows or slings. Some auxiliary units were made up of men required to fight for Rome as part of a treaty agreement between their people and the empire. In any case, up until about the middle of the second century CE, auxiliaries rarely served in their home province. So, for example, the soldiers who kept order for the empire in Britain were from what are now the Netherlands, northeastern Greece, Algeria, and Ukraine.

Roman rule brought order and peace to conquered areas, but at a price. Many thought this price was too high, although few had the courage to speak out. Roman soldiers were never far away, ready to deal with troublemakers at a moment's notice. But in the 80s CE, the empire met strong resistance when it tried to push its rule into northern Britain. The historian Tacitus put the following speech into the mouth of a British leader named Calgacus, rallying his warriors against the Romans in what is now northeastern Scotland:

> Up until this day, we who live in this last strip of land and last home of liberty have been protected by our very remoteness. But now the farthest limits of Britain have been opened up … Beyond us, there are no tribes, nothing except waves and rocks and, more dangerous than these, the Romans, whose oppression you have in vain tried to escape by obedience and submission. Plunderers of the world they are, and now that there is no more territory left to occupy their hands which have already laid the world waste, they are scouring the seas. If the enemy is rich, they are greedy; if the enemy is poor, they are power-hungry … Alone of all men they covet rich nations and poor nations with equal passion. They rob, they slaughter, they plunder—and they call it "empire." Where they make a waste-land, they call it "peace."
>
> Nature has planned that each man love his children and family very dearly. Yet these are torn from us … to be slaves elsewhere … Our possessions and our money are consumed in providing **tribute**; our farmland and our yearly produce are consumed in providing them with grain; our very bodies and hands are worn down while clearing forests and swamps for them, who beat and insult us.

When auxiliaries and legionnaires were discharged from the army, they often settled in towns or farming communities in the province where they were stationed. This was one of the most important ways that Roman culture spread through the countryside of conquered territories.

# Chapter Two

# Rural Lifestyles

Mare Germanicum

Oceanus Atlanticus

Britannia

Belgica

Germania Superior

Lugdunensis

Noricum

Aquitania

Raetia

Pannonia

Narbonensis

Italia

Daci

Dalmatia

M

Tarraconensis

Corsica

•Roma

Macedoni

Lusitania

Sardinia

Epirus

Baetica

Sicilia

Africa

Mauretania

Mare Internur

Cyrer

This map shows the empire's landmass at its peak. The majority of Rome's population lived in rural areas.

Country life in ancient Rome was defined by hard work. Yet beyond this unifying theme, individuals living in the countryside had vastly different experiences. Social class shaped much of an individual's lifestyle in ancient Rome, as did the kind of rural community they were a part of. Rural Romans lived in villages or on the frontier. Others lived as nomads, and wealthy Romans maintained luxurious villas as a means of escaping the city.

Environments were similarly varied. Britain was damp and chilly, North Africa hot and dry. Germany was heavily wooded; in Greece, the terrain was rough and rocky. Along the Nile River in Egypt, the flat, fertile land was perfect for growing wheat; Italian hillsides were covered with grapevines and olive trees. In Spain, the earth held rich deposits of gold and other metals, while marble could be quarried from many parts of Asia Minor.

# A Closer Look at Cato

Marcus Portius Cato was born in 234 BCE to a farmer and his wife. Cato remained interested in agriculture his entire life, though his successes in the Second Punic War laid the foundation for a career in politics that led him far away from the family farm. Cato was characterized by his stubbornness. For instance, he believed that the Carthaginians posed a threat to Rome even after the Romans defeated them in the Second Punic War—and the

Cato the Elder lived from 234 BCE to 149 BCE.

Carthaginians' resulting integration into the empire. Therefore, he ended every speech he gave to the Senate (his recorded speeches number more than 150) with the words "Carthage must be destroyed," no matter the topic he was speaking about.

Cato also held strong beliefs about the proper way to run a farm, so he wrote an eighty-page treatise titled *On Agriculture*. This book is important because it sheds light on the way farms were run in ancient Rome and also because it is one of the oldest surviving Latin texts. Cato's book was influential in his day, too. Columella's book about agriculture, also called *On Agriculture*, was inspired by Cato's treatise.

Cato died in 149 BCE. Cato's great-grandson of the same name followed in his great-grandfather's footsteps, becoming a noted politician in his own right. To distinguish between the two, historians refer to the men as "Cato the Elder" and "Cato the Younger," respectively. Sometimes you'll also see Cato the Elder called "Cato the Censor" after his elected position.

## Village Life

Many country people lived in villages. Some rural settlements might have only a handful of houses, occupied by farm families that worked the surrounding fields. Other villages might be home not only to farmers but also to craftspeople, and there might be an inn and other amenities. Pliny mentioned in a letter to one of his friends that the village near his seaside villa had three public bathhouses.

Small towns were also important to the countryside. Farmers could sell some of their produce at markets in these towns and could use the money to buy things that they couldn't make themselves or get from village craftspeople.

In much of the Roman Empire, villages were often made up entirely of native people living in their traditional ways. For instance, the first four books of the New Testament of the Bible frequently describe village life in the province of Judaea (roughly located in modern Israel), where fishing was an important part of the rural economy. Throughout the empire, there could be a good deal of variety even in the basic layout of country communities: as an example, many British villages were surrounded by wide ditches, while North African villages were often walled and fortified with towers.

## Frontier Life

Roman legions were headquartered in leading provincial cities. Soldiers, however—both legionnaires and auxiliaries—manned outposts and forts that were strung through the countryside or along the empire's boundaries. One such frontier was Hadrian's Wall, which divided the province of Britannia (Britain) from what is now Scotland. Built into the wall were sixteen or seventeen fortresses, each manned by some five hundred auxiliaries. There were also watchtowers every third of a mile (0.5 kilometers) and fortified gateways,

Archaeological excavations of Hadrian's Wall continue today.

called milecastles, roughly every 1 mile (1.6 km). Each milecastle could house a garrison of around thirty men.

Wherever soldiers were stationed, villages soon came into being. Some local people wanted the protection of the Roman soldiers, for in many places bandits and raiders threatened the safety of the countryside. Others were more interested in earning money by supplying the soldiers with goods and services. Until 197 CE, rank-and-file legionnaires and auxiliaries were not allowed to marry, but often they had unofficial wives who, with their children, naturally wanted to live as close to the army camp as possible. So a typical settlement near a military base might include a tavern, a few craftspeople's workshops, a marketplace, and the homes of soldiers' families and of people who farmed the surrounding countryside. Over time, many such settlements grew into full-fledged towns and cities.

## NOBLE LANDHOLDERS

In both Italy and the provinces, large tracts of land were owned by the emperor—and all of Egypt belonged to him. Each of the emperor's estates was run by an official called a **procurator**, who was often a freed slave. The procurator usually rented out parts of the estate to **tenant farmers**. Sometimes extensive parcels of land were rented to one person. This "lessee-in-chief" or chief tenant would be allowed to have part of the estate farmed for himself, and he would sublet the rest to humbler tenant farmers. The emperor's estates often incorporated entire villages, as this inscription from North Africa shows:

> Anyone living within the estate of Villa Magna Variana, that is, in the village of Siga, is permitted to bring those fields which are unsurveyed under cultivation … Of the crops produced on such land they [the tenants] must in accordance with the Mancian Law deliver shares … to the chief lessees or **bailiffs** of this estate as follows … one-third of the wheat from the threshing floor, one-third of the barley from the threshing floor, one-fourth of the beans from the threshing floor, one-third of the wine from the vat, one-third of the oil extracted, one sextarius [a little more than 1 pint or 0.5 liters] of honey per hive.

Other wealthy Romans also had great landholdings—it is said that at one point, half the province of Africa (roughly, modern Tunisia) was owned by six men. This was an extreme case, however, and most estates were not so vast. Large landowners generally lived in the cities, not on their estates. But on most estates they would have a villa, which they visited from time to time. Many wealthy Romans had a network of villas throughout Italy so that they and their friends would have places to stay while traveling, since there were few decent hotels. The estates themselves were run by stewards or bailiffs and worked by

Roman roads connected urban areas to the rural areas that provided the empire with food.

slaves, tenant farmers, **sharecroppers**, or some combination of these. Italian estates produced mainly wine, olive oil, and grain, but in some parts of the peninsula great tracts of land were devoted to cattle ranching.

The poet Horace had a fairly modest estate about 30 miles (48 km) from Rome, and he spent as much time in his villa there as he could. He rented part of his estate to five tenant farmers, each family living in its own cottage and working a plot of land. The rest of the estate was worked by eight slaves, overseen by a foreman. Its produce (including the profits from sales) directly supported the poet. He had grain fields, a vegetable garden, an orchard, a vineyard, an olive grove, a wood, pastureland, and cattle, sheep, and goats. The countryside around Horace's estate was still quite wild: once while rambling alone in the forest, he unexpectedly came upon a wolf—luckily for both, the poet was unarmed, and the wolf soon went its own way.

## NOMADS

Not all rural people lived in villages, on villas, or near military posts. In almost every province there were at least some **freeholders** who occupied scattered or isolated farmsteads, working land that often had been passed down through families for generations. And in North Africa and a few other areas on the empire's edges, many groups carried on an age-old nomadic lifestyle. They traveled from place to place, following the grazing patterns of their animals. At the same time, they played a role in village culture by trading products from their herds for grain, vegetables, and the like. In addition, nomads provided temporary, seasonal labor on many farms.

## DIFFERENT PEOPLE, DIFFERENT EXPERIENCES

As we've seen, the diversity of the rural experience makes it nearly impossible to generalize about rural Romans. A nomad's daily life would have been unrecognizable to a wealthy landowner visiting his villa. However, the many communities dotting the Roman countryside worked together to support the empire. In the next chapter, we'll take an in-depth look at housing in ancient Rome.

# CHAPTER THREE

# COUNTRY HOMES

The walls of this once lavish Roman villa still stand on Portuguese farmland.

*"A good piece of land will please you more at each visit."*

—Cato

Just like today, architecture in the ancient world was a blend of engineering, manual labor, and art. Romans were major innovators in the field as evidenced by their contributions (concrete and the arch, for example) and their writing on the topic. One of the most important texts from ancient Rome is called *The Ten Books on Architecture*. Marcus Vitruvius Pollio wrote the books to help the architects of his time. Vitruvius noted that the native people in different parts of the empire each had traditional building styles.

## MODEST LIVING QUARTERS

Houses in what are now France and Spain, Vitruvius said, were roofed with oak shingles or thatch. On the south coast of the Black Sea, tall log cabins were typical. "On the other hand," Vitruvius continued:

the Phrygians [of central Asia Minor], who live in an open country, have no forests and consequently lack timber. They therefore select a natural hillock, run a trench through the middle of it, dig passages, and extend the interior space as widely as the site admits. Over it they build a pyramidal roof of logs fastened together, and this they cover with reeds and brushwood, heaping up very high mounds of earth above their dwellings. Thus their fashion in houses makes their winters very warm and their summers very cool.

We know from other evidence that British houses were often round and constructed of **wattle and daub**, with steep, conical thatched roofs. Egyptian villagers built their homes of mud brick, with flat roofs. The Romans rarely interfered with these various building traditions, but in their own settlements, whether in Italy or the provinces, they built in their own style.

Roman country houses were mainly rectangular in shape. They might be constructed of stone, wood, concrete with a brick facing, or a combination of these materials. Roofs were usually covered with clay tiles. The poorest homes had floors of hard-packed earth; people who were more comfortably off had wood, stone, or tile underfoot. Walls were often plastered or whitewashed inside and out.

A simple home or cottage was typically partitioned into a few small rooms, one leading into another. Archaeologists in Italy have found the remains of a humble farmhouse with an interior measuring approximately 33 feet by 15 feet (10 meters by 4.5 meters). There is evidence that farm animals sheltered in one part of the house—a common living arrangement in many places in the past. The animals were protected from thieves and the weather, and when it was cold, their body heat helped warm the house for the human residents.

The majority of country people had only a few simple furnishings: at most, probably a bed or couch, a storage chest, a table, a bench or two, a cupboard, some large clay storage jars, and a handmill for grinding grain. The kitchen area had a raised open hearth and, sometimes, an oven. To cook over the hearth fire, people would use a griddle, a spit for roasting meat (when it was available), and in some areas a cauldron hung on a tripod. In a small cottage, the hearth fire was the only source of heat. It also created a lot of smoke, which escaped through an open door or window, or through holes in the roof. Windows could be closed with wooden shutters, or they may have been covered with oiled paper or a thin sheet of animal skin. The only artificial light came from oil lamps or, in areas that did not raise olives, candles made of beeswax or animal fat.

On most farms, there would be other buildings in addition to the house. The number and type of outbuildings depended on how well off the family was and what they were raising. If the farm was prosperous, there could be a separate structure for the kitchen, a bathhouse, workshops for making olive oil and wine, storage buildings, and stables. Many such farms were arranged around a rectangular farmyard, with the house on one side and the additional buildings set along two other sides.

## Rural Retreats

Although Horace once claimed, "In a poor cottage you may live a better life than kings and the friends of kings," his own country home was far from a cottage. Archaeologists have been exploring the site and the remains of Horace's villa for many years. Together with a large formal garden, it took up an area roughly the size of a football field. The entrance led directly into the garden, which had a pool at the center and was surrounded on all four sides by a covered walkway. At the back of the garden was the door into the house. The first room was an **atrium**, which would have been used as a living room and a place to welcome visitors. It was open to the sky, allowing in light and fresh air.

Bedrooms were located off the atrium. More rooms, including a dining room, were arranged around a courtyard at the back of the villa. In addition, there was a private bathhouse that could be reached from the garden walkway.

An atrium

# Villas of All Kinds

When classicists discuss lavish villas in ancient Rome, they are usually referring to a *villa urbana*. These villas were the country homes of Roman elite located outside of city limits. However, there were several kinds of villas, each with its own name:

*Villae maritimae*: villas near the ocean

*Villae suburbanae*: villas close to a city

*Villae rusticae*: villas with a farm

It was not unusual for a landowner to build a villa urbana and a villa rustica on the same property. In this circumstance, the villa urbana was the home of the landowner, and the villa rustica was the home of his slaves and other laborers. These different types of villas could be found throughout Rome—including the far reaches of the empire. Archaeologists have even discovered villae martimae in Africa, although the surviving sites date to a time slightly after the peak of the empire.

Some scholars argue that even more nuanced categories of villas existed. These scholars warn against trying to classify villas according to simple terms.

Horace's country home was considered quite a modest place in comparison with those of many rich people. The walls of Pliny's seaside villa, for instance, enclosed more than forty rooms and outdoor areas. These included an atrium; bedrooms for himself, his slaves, and guests; four dining rooms, each looking out on a different view; storage rooms for grain and wine; a ball court; an exercise area; a sunroom; a study; two courtyards; an herb garden; a large garden with a covered walkway and a small vineyard; and a terrace, as Pliny wrote to a friend in a letter that proudly and lovingly described his seaside retreat. He was trying to persuade this friend to come visit him, so along with portraying the villa's beautiful setting, he made sure to mention his home's conveniences: baths, pools, and a room for massages were just a few.

Wealthy Romans appreciated their comforts, and they loved to be surrounded by art, especially in their country homes. Walls would be decorated with richly colored **frescoes**—or paintings—of landscapes, mythological scenes, or decorative designs. The floors were ornamented with **mosaics**,

This mosaic is part of the permanent collection at the Museo Nazionale Romano in Rome.

pictures or patterns made from small squares of stone. Some mosaics were in black and white, while others were in many colors. The furniture was of the highest quality. When wealthy people ate, they reclined on cushioned dining couches—three set around a low table—often in their gardens. The gardens themselves were enhanced by statues, fountains, and shrubs trimmed into various shapes, such as animals, words, ships, and even hunting scenes.

The water supply for rich and poor country dwellers alike usually came from wells and nearby springs, streams, or rivers. The wealthy, of course, enjoyed luxuries that were not available to others—for example, the rich could cover their windows with sheets of transparent mica or, more rarely, glass. Some very prosperous people had an underfloor heating system called a hypocaust. Otherwise, they generally relied on charcoal **braziers** for extra heat in their many rooms. The charcoal smoldered smokily, and to feel the brazier's warmth a person had to be almost right next to it. In winter, therefore, the rich might be almost as cold as the poor. They also made do with the same limited sources of artificial light—although wealthy people had ornate lampstands and candelabras and could afford to use more oil and candles than poor people could.

## How to Set Up Your Villa

Columella wrote *On Agriculture* during the first century CE. In this work, Columella gave advice about how to run a large estate. Here are some selections:

> The size of a villa or housing structure should be determined by the total area of the farm; and the villa should be divided into three sections: one section resembling a city home [for the landowner], one section like a real farmhouse [for the workers and livestock], and the third section for storing farm products.

Now in the farmhouse part of the villa there should be a large kitchen with a high ceiling … so that the wood beams may be secure against the danger of fire … The best plan will be to construct the cells for unchained slaves facing south. For those in chains let there be an underground prison, as healthful as possible … For livestock there should be, within the villa, stalls which are not subject to either cold or heat. For draft and pack animals there should be two sets of stalls, winter ones and summer ones … Cells for oxherds and shepherds should be placed next to their animals so that running out to care for them may be convenient …

The third part of the villa, that designated for storing produce, is divided into rooms for oil, for oil and wine presses, for aged wine, and for wine not yet fermented; into lofts for hay and straw; and into areas for warehouses and granaries … The wine room is placed on the ground floor; but it should be far removed from the bathrooms, the oven, the manure pile, and other filthy areas giving off a foul stench.

Columella had plenty more to say on the topic of running a farm. *On Agriculture* is twelve volumes long!

## COUNTRY HOUSES, BIG AND SMALL

Country houses in ancient Rome ranged from opulent to rustic. (In fact, the word "rustic" comes from a Latin word related to country living.) Today, it's fun to imagine life in a lavish villa with beautiful views of the empire. And we don't just have to imagine what it would be like—archaeological sites still exist today, providing classicists with a glimpse into the past.

# A Closer Look at Columella and Varro

Lucius Junius Moderatus Columella was born sometime in the first century CE. Historians believe that Columella served in the army for a short time and then spent the remainder of his life as a farmer; while Columella's writing has been passed down through the ages, biographical information has not. In addition to writing *On Agriculture*, Columella penned another book series

Varro lived from 116 BCE to 27 BCE.

about farming that has been lost. Columella is often discussed alongside Cato and Varro. It is clear from citations in Columella's writing that he had read their work.

Marcus Terentius Varro was born in 116 BCE. As a young man, Varro received a comprehensive education and is often noted for the depth of his knowledge. Varro ultimately became an author and a politician. He wrote hundreds of books—Varro himself put the number at over four hundred, though scholars now believe the number is closer to six hundred. (Experts point out that Roman manuscripts were much shorter than books today.) Yet the only complete surviving text by Varro is *Farm Topics*. Portions of Varro's other work remain, too. Varro's book *On the Latin Language* is considered to be an important work of scholarship.

# CHAPTER FOUR

# ON THE
# FARM

Excavations in France unearthed these
Roman farming tools.

*"Nowadays farmwork is done by feet which have
been chained, by hands which have been punished,
by faces which have been branded ..."*
—Cincinnatus on the role of slaves in farming

In ancient Rome, farm tools included scythes, hoes, and hand shovels. Of course, these tools all have one important factor in common: they require laborers to do the heavy lifting. Animals like donkeys and oxen pulled plows and turned millstones, but successful farms depended on humans using hand tools. In order to staff their farms, landowners relied heavily on slaves.

## Slave Labor

Wealthy landowners generally worked in the city in business and government. Rural property was an investment for them, a major source of wealth, but they very rarely took part in the actual work of the countryside. Of course, there were always a few landowners like Horace, who came to feel that he could only do his real work (writing poetry) in the peace of his farm. The poet wrote that he even enjoyed getting his hands dirty from time to time.

This mosaic shows the labor required to harvest grapes.

The future emperor Marcus Aurelius, too, thought that country chores could occasionally be fun, and he detailed the joy he found working on one of his family's estates in a letter to his tutor. By and large, though, rural work was for the poor and unprivileged.

Much of the labor on farms was done by slaves. Estate owners might have a great many; freeholders and tenant farmers, too, often had some slaves to help them with their work. Slavery was a fact of Roman life, as it was in most ancient civilizations. When the empire made new conquests, large numbers of war captives were enslaved. Slaves were also bought and sold in markets, many of which were located in Asia Minor. Children born to slaves automatically became slaves themselves. Sometimes referred to as "home-grown" slaves, they made up a large portion of the empire's enslaved population.

Uniquely for their time, the Romans very often freed their slaves. Freed slaves became Roman citizens, and their children could advance in society and even, occasionally, hold political office. Most rural slaves, however, did not enjoy such good fortune. Slaves who were freed were typically from the eastern part of the empire and worked in their owner's household, where he or she got to know them personally. Enslaved farm laborers, unless they were "home grown," were generally from **barbarian** areas, such as Britain and Germany. Such slaves were unlikely to have a knowledge of Latin or Greek, or of the culture of the Mediterranean world. Moreover, they seldom came into contact with their masters. For these reasons, slaves who labored on large estates were almost never freed.

Farm slaves worked extremely hard, and they could be severely punished for any kind of disobedience. On some estates, owners kept unruly slaves chained together; they worked the fields as chain gangs during the day, and at night they were locked in a prison. Pliny, however, assured one of his friends in a letter that he didn't keep his slaves chained. And Columella recommended that a master should personally make sure his slaves had decent food, clothing, and living conditions; should talk and even joke around with them; should allow them to complain about cruel treatment and then take action against it; and should reward especially good workers. All the same, many rural slaves endured very inhumane conditions. An example is found in this description of the often-beaten laborers at a flour mill, written by the second-century North African author Apuleius:

> Their skin was striped all over with livid scourge-scars; their wealed backs were crusted rather than clothed with their patchwork rags; some had no more covering than a bit of dangled apron; and every shirt was

so tattered that the body was visible through the rents. Their brows were branded; their heads were half-shaved; irons clanked on their feet; their faces were sallow and ugly; the smoky gloom of the reeking overheated room had bleared and dulled their smarting eyes; and … their faces were wanly smeared with the dirty flour.

## Work for All Seasons

The realities of slave labor were far from the mind of Virgil when he wrote loving descriptions of a farm's seasonal cycle. In fact, Virgil's poems about farming, the *Georgics*, never mention slavery at all. In his time and in the parts of Italy where he lived, small farms worked by free men were probably the norm. But although freeholders, tenant farmers, and sharecroppers did not suffer the cruelties of slavery, they still endured many hardships and long hours to raise their animals and produce their crops. There was always work to be done, whatever the weather and season.

Wheat growing in modern-day Tuscany

Naturally, the year's agricultural activities varied from place to place, depending on climate and environment. In Italy, the farming year began in March, when grape vines were pruned and wheat was sown. By May, the grain plants were well established, and the furrows where they grew had to be weeded and hoed. This was also the month for shearing sheep and washing wool. And before the coming of summer's heat, conscientious farmers fertilized their fields and orchards with manure and compost.

June was the time for cutting grass to dry for hay, which farm animals would eat during the winter. In July, farmers harvested barley and beans. In August, the wheat was ripe, and it had to be harvested without delay, before the crop could be destroyed by birds, rodents, or storms. After harvesting, the grain had to be dried, then threshed to break the head of grain from the straw, then winnowed to finish cleaning the grain of seed coatings and other chaff. Threshing and winnowing could go on for months—these tasks were fitted in whenever there was a break from other farm chores.

September saw the ripening of various fruits, and preparations were made for the vintage, or grape harvest, which came in October. Some grapes were selected for eating fresh, but most were destined to be turned into wine. This was a lengthy process, which began with pressing the juice out of the grapes. They were placed on a raised floor in a press room, where barefooted workers trod on them. Grooves or channels in the floor allowed the juice to run out into containers. A mechanical press might be used to get the remaining juice out of the grape pulp. The grape juice then fermented in large jars, barrels, or vats, until the wine was ready. Some estates produced a tremendous amount of wine—archaeologists estimate that on one 300-acre (120-hectare) estate in central Italy, more than 250,000 gallons (950,000 liters) were made a year.

# Virgil's *Georgics*

Unlike the agricultural writing of Cato, Varro, and Columella, Virgil's famous work about rural life was a series of poems—the *Georgics*. Publius Vergilius Maro (known as "Virgil" and "Vergil" in English) was born in 70 BCE. He was reclusive, preferring to write poetry in the countryside to life in the capital city of Rome, where he had studied as a young man. Virgil's *Georgics* are known for offering practical advice about farming as well as boasting verses that marvel at nature. More than two thousand lines of poetry comprise the *Georgics*.

Virgil is better known today as the author of the *Aeneid*, however. Modern audiences still turn to this epic poem, and it cemented Virgil as one of Rome's greatest poets. Though the *Aeneid* was unfinished when Virgil died in 19 BCE, the work was wildly popular with readers around the empire. Historians Lesley and Roy A. Adkins note that Virgil's writing left a surprising legacy:

> After his death his fame increased to the point of superstitious reverence. The *Sortes Vergiliannae* (*Virgilian Lots*) were attempts to prophesy the future by opening his books and picking a line at random, widely practiced from Hadrian's time.

Virgil lived from 70 BCE to 19 BCE.

In November, farmers planted winter wheat and barley. December was the month for fertilizing grape vines, planting beans, and cutting wood. Moreover, olives were now ripe and ready to pick. They had to be handled carefully. Some olives were intended to be eaten, but most were pressed to make olive oil. Both the grape and olive harvests required many extra workers, so landowners or farm managers would hire local people or, in some parts of the empire, nomads to help out.

After all of this, farmers got a bit of a rest in January. They cut willow branches and reeds for basketmaking and other uses, repaired tools, and the like. Then in February it was time to start tending the grapevines and weed the grain fields, getting them ready for the next planting.

## OTHER OCCUPATIONS

While most people in the countryside worked at farming, rural areas also had some craftspeople, such as carpenters and blacksmiths; service workers, such as innkeepers and bakers; and what we would call professionals, particularly doctors and veterinarians. These people might be part of the labor force on a large estate, or they might live in a village and be available to anyone in the surrounding area.

A great many herders, in some parts of the empire, lived apart from village and estate life for much of the year. In spring, they drove huge flocks of sheep or goats, or herds of cattle, up into mountain pastures, and there they stayed until autumn. This was a hard, lonely, and even dangerous existence. The herders followed their animals over steep and difficult terrain and were outdoors all day in all kinds of weather, with only little huts for shelter. As Varro wrote, "The type of man selected for this work should be strong, swift, agile and supple of limb; men who, as well as following the flock, can also defend it against wild beasts and robbers; men able to lift loads on to the backs of pack-animals, to dash out ahead, and to hurl **javelins**."

In coastal areas and around rivers and lakes, fishing was often more important than farming or herding. Some fishermen owned their own boats and equipment. Others might lease vessels and gear from someone else, in exchange for money or part of the catch. Seaside villas often included fish farms, with one or more tanks for breeding fish.

Mining was the major activity in many rural districts. Most miners were slaves or convicts, and their lives were miserable.

## BOUNTIFUL HARVESTS?

Farmers' yields depended on a number of factors: the size of their farm, the types of crops planted, and weather conditions. Perhaps the most important factor was the help they had planting and harvesting. As we've seen, it took workers of all kinds to run a farm in ancient Rome—just like today. In the next chapter, we'll explore what life was like for Roman men in the countryside.

# CHAPTER FIVE

# RUGGED MEN

A statue of the Roman folk hero
Cincinnatus in Cincinnati, Ohio

"Remember that a farm is like a man—however great the income, if there is extravagance but little is left."

—Cato

Ancient Rome was a man's world—and this held true in both the city, where elite men made laws and ruled the empire, and the country, where farms were owned and run by men. Yet from the first century BCE on, writers frequently complained respect for the head of the household was diminishing in the cities. In the country, on the other hand, the traditional values were said to be alive and well. It is hard for us now to tell whether or not that common opinion was true, for farmers and farmworkers almost never wrote about themselves.

Of course, not all country men were of the landholding elite. The countryside was home to tenant farmers, sharecroppers, male laborers, and slaves, too. These men led very different lives in rural locations around the empire. We can assume, however, that all rural men carried on with such Roman virtues as toughness, perseverance, and hard work—not as an ideal, but because these qualities were necessary for survival.

## Proud Landowners

Generation after generation of Romans learned the story of Cincinnatus, a role model of ideal manhood. In 458 BCE, he was out plowing his fields when members of the Roman Senate came to beg him to take command of the army. Cincinnatus did not hesitate to do his duty, and he led the army to a swift victory. Sixteen days later, he resigned his command and returned to his little cottage, his fields, and his plowing. Recalling the stories of Cincinnatus and other farmer-heroes, Columella wrote in the first century CE:

> I am reminded by the great number of written records that our ancestors regarded attention to farming as a matter of pride … I realize that the manners and strenuous lifestyle of bygone days are out of favour with present-day extravagance … All of us who are heads of families have abandoned the sickle and the plough, and slunk inside the city.

Of course, Columella was thinking only of upper-class heads of families. But one reason that he wrote his book on agriculture was to convince some of these men of the economic opportunities of farming. He wanted landowners, even if they didn't work their estates with their own hands, to at least have a thorough knowledge of the principles of agriculture and farm management. That way they could appoint the right kind of men as bailiffs and foremen, they could make sound decisions about land usage and the like, and their estates would be as productive—and profitable—as possible.

Pliny the Younger was one landowner who took his responsibilities quite seriously. In a letter to a friend, he asked advice about whether or not he should buy a certain piece of property. On another occasion, Pliny wrote to the emperor Trajan requesting a thirty-day leave of absence from his government duties so that he could go out to the countryside to settle some problems on one of his estates.

Several of Pliny's letters described not the responsibilities but the pleasures of owning country property. He wrote of the leisure time he enjoyed when visiting his various villas. He slept as late as he wanted in the morning and lay about for a while, thinking and then dictating letters or literary works to his secretary. A few hours later, he went out and sat on the terrace to meditate and dictate some more. Then it was time for a carriage or horseback ride, followed by a nap. After that, he might read aloud from a Greek or Latin speech. This would be followed by a walk, some exercise, and a bath. While he ate dinner with his wife and a few others, a slave often read a book to them. Then everyone would enjoy some music or a dramatic reading of a comedy. Before bed, Pliny took one more walk, along with some of his better-educated slaves, enjoying their conversation. This, he wrote, was his favorite routine, but sometimes it varied. He might join a hunting party (although he took writing materials with him and usually worked on something literary while others pursued the quarry), or friends might drop by for a visit. And, of course, now and then he had to devote his attention to his tenant farmers and their complaints.

## TENANT FARMERS AND SHARECROPPERS

In one of his letters, Pliny told a friend that on some of his lands the tenants had gotten so far behind in paying their rents that they would never be able to catch up. Pliny decided that the best solution to this problem would be to sharecrop. These tenants were lucky that Pliny was willing to try a new arrangement with them. In many cases, when a tenant got behind in paying his rent, the landowner would seize and sell his equipment, slaves, livestock, and

# Hunting and Fishing

One draw of life in the countryside was the opportunity to hunt. Roman men hunted deer and boars for meat. They also hunted predators to prevent them from attacking livestock; bears could be cause for concern, as could wild dogs. According to Virgil, who was probably thinking about the farmers of northern Italy, wintertime in particular brought opportunities for relaxation, enjoying company, and hunting:

> Winter's the tenant's rest.
> In the cold weather farmers mostly enjoy their gains,
> happily occupied in giving mutual parties.
> The genial winter's invitation frees from care …
> But even so then is the time to gather acorns
> and bay-berries and olives and the blood-red myrtle;
> time to set snares for game-birds and nets for the stag
> and to pursue the long-eared hare; time to shoot deer,
> whirling the hempen thongs of a Balearic sling,
> when snow lies deep, when rivers hustle ice along.

Fishing was another means of introducing diversity into the rural diet. Not only did Romans fish in oceans, ponds, and streams, wealthy Romans sometimes started their own fish farms. Scholars believe that these fish farms were somewhat unusual because they were expensive to maintain.

Boar hunting was memorialized in other verses by Virgil.

seed grain. This brought the tenant up to date on his rent in the short term—but he no longer had the resources to farm his holding.

Tenants on private estates typically leased their land for five years at a time. A wise landowner generally preferred to rent a holding to the same tenant over and over; the tenant would tend to think of the land almost as his own and so would take better care of it. When he died, the lease might even pass to his son. The emperors came to encourage a similar stability on their estates. From the reign of Hadrian in the first part of the second century CE, an imperial tenant who brought new land into cultivation was guaranteed this land for the rest of his life. If he planted a fig orchard or vineyard, he could even have the land rent free for five years; planting an olive orchard earned him ten years without rent.

Unlike wealthy landowners, tenant farmers and sharecroppers had very few opportunities for leisure. There were holidays, of course, when they did not work. Sometimes bad weather would give them a break from the heaviest outdoor chores. Then they might spend their time making baskets or nets, or mending tools. While engaged in such activities, they could also enjoy conversation and storytelling with family and friends.

## MEN AT WORK

Upper-class men were expected to lead useful lives serving the public, participating in politics and government, or managing vast business interests. So perhaps it is no wonder that upper-class poets often portrayed country life as an escape from reality. However, it seems clear that for most men, life in the country was not a retreat. The following chapter looks at women's experience in rural Rome.

This mosaic is now part of the Jamahiriya Museum's collection in Libya.

# CHAPTER SIX

# STRONG WOMEN

Scholars debate the identity of the maternal figure shown here, yet many say that she is Tellus, the goddess of the earth.

> *"But be the bailiff what he may, he should be given a woman companion to keep him within bounds and yet in certain matters to be a help to him."*
>
> *—Columella*

In Roman culture, a woman's main tasks in life were to marry, to care for her husband and his home, and to bear children to be his heirs. Fulfilling these roles, she was expected to uphold such traditional virtues as modesty, respectability, faithfulness, conscientiousness, and thriftiness. These ideals originated in Rome, and they spread to the upper classes throughout the empire. People living in rural communities in many provinces, however, often kept more to their own traditions. In some places, therefore, women had more rights and status than in Italy, but in other places they had fewer.

## THE LEGAL STATUS OF WOMEN

Under Roman law, free women did not enjoy the same status as free men. A woman nearly always had a male guardian—her father, husband, or another relative. In the case of a freedwoman, her guardian was generally her former master. The guardian was supposed to advise the woman on all her legal and financial dealings. Some guardians, however, gave their wards considerable freedom to make their own decisions. And a freeborn woman who bore three children was released from guardianship; four children earned a freedwoman the same privilege.

With or without guardians, though, women were still allowed to buy, sell, own, and inherit land. Pliny's letters give us two examples: In one, he offered to sell some of his lakefront property in northern Italy to a woman friend. In another, he wrote to the manager of the farm that he had given to his old nurse, urging him to make the farm as profitable as possible so that the nurse would have a good living. Another example comes from a town in what is now Tunisia, where one of the area's major landowners in the second century CE was a woman named Valeria Atticilla. We also know that women owned luxurious seaside villas on the Bay of Naples, south of Rome.

## FAMILIAL ROLES

Girls married as young as eleven or twelve; by the age of thirty, a woman might well be a grandmother. A great many women, however, did not live that long. Childbirth was very difficult and dangerous in the ancient world. This tombstone inscription from what is now Hungary tells a common story:

> Here I lie, a **matron** named Veturia … I lived for twenty-seven years, and I was married for sixteen years to the same man. After I gave birth to six children, only one of whom is still alive, I died. Titus Julius Fortunatus, a soldier of Legion II Adiutrix, provided this memorial for his wife, who was incomparable and showed outstanding devotion to him.

In memorials like this one, a husband often expressed his feelings for his dead wife, praising her virtues and the harmony of their marriage. Sometimes wives set up similar memorials for their husbands. Judging from these inscriptions and other sources, the ideal marriage was one where the couple lived together in peace, contentment, and mutual respect. Romantic love was perhaps not as important—since most marriages were arranged, the couple might not even know each other very well before their wedding. But often love grew over time.

## WOMEN AT WORK

An upper-class woman did very little work other than supervising her slaves. Traditionally, though, women of every class spent much of their time spinning, weaving, and sewing. This was true of nearly all women in the countryside.

Like rural women in most times and places, tenant farmers' wives probably did many farm chores. The bulk of their activity, though, likely involved preserving and preparing food, along with making cloth and clothing. Women slaves in the countryside did a variety of work, caring for farm animals and laboring in the fields, but Columella recommended that on cold or rainy days they instead do woolwork. For slaves, this would include cleaning and carding the wool as well as spinning it into thread.

Some female slaves accompanied shepherds up to the mountain pastures. These women, Varro explained, "can follow the flocks, prepare the shepherds' meals, and make the men more attentive to their work." He added that when he visited what is now Bosnia, he observed that the women there "are as good workers as the men . . . they can either do the shepherding, or bring logs for the fire and cook the food, or look after the farm implements [tools] in the huts."

# Barbarian Women

In some areas that the Romans conquered, women had a higher status than in the Mediterranean world. In fact, among the people whom Greeks and Romans referred to as barbarians, women could hold positions of great influence, even becoming political and religious leaders. Tacitus wrote that German warriors valued the praise of the women of their families more than any other praise. When injured, men went to their mothers and wives to have their wounds healed. According to tradition, sometimes when men were near to losing a battle, women's constant urging gave them the inspiration and strength to win victory after all.

A monument to Boudicca in London

The most famous British leader of Roman times was Boudicca, queen of the Iceni tribe in eastern Britain. In 61 CE, she led a rebellion that nearly succeeded in driving the Romans out of Britain entirely. Though little biographical information remains about her, the Roman author Dio Cassius included a description of her intimidating physical appearance in his history of Rome.

The most important female slave on a large estate was the forewoman, who was the foreman's companion and assistant. (Usually they had a relationship like husband and wife, but slaves were not allowed to be legally married.) The forewoman's duties were wide ranging. This selection from Columella's book covers just a portion of them:

At one moment she will have to go to the loom and teach the weavers whatever she knows better than them … At another moment, she will have to check on those slaves who are preparing the food for the familia [household]. Then she will also have to see that the kitchen, cowsheds, and even the stables are cleaned. And she will also have to open up the sick-rooms occasionally, even if they are empty of patients, and keep them free of dirt … She will, in addition, have to be in attendance when the stewards of the pantry and cellar are weighing something, and also be present when the shepherds are milking in the stables … But she will also certainly need to be present when the sheep are sheared, and to examine the wool carefully.

A rural slave woman's other major duty was to give birth to children, who would be the property of the master; "home-grown" slaves were generally considered to be the best workers. Columella wrote that he rewarded slave women who bore several children. A woman who had three children was exempted from work (other than caring for the children, we assume). If she had four or more, she was given her freedom. The children, however, remained slaves.

## A Challenging Existence

Though upper-class women had plenty of help on their estates, the majority of women in the countryside led challenging lives. Sometimes their lives were downright dangerous: many women did not survive childbirth at a time when medical care was nearly nonexistent and would appear unrecognizable to us today. In the next chapter, we'll see that childhood also looked very different in ancient Rome.

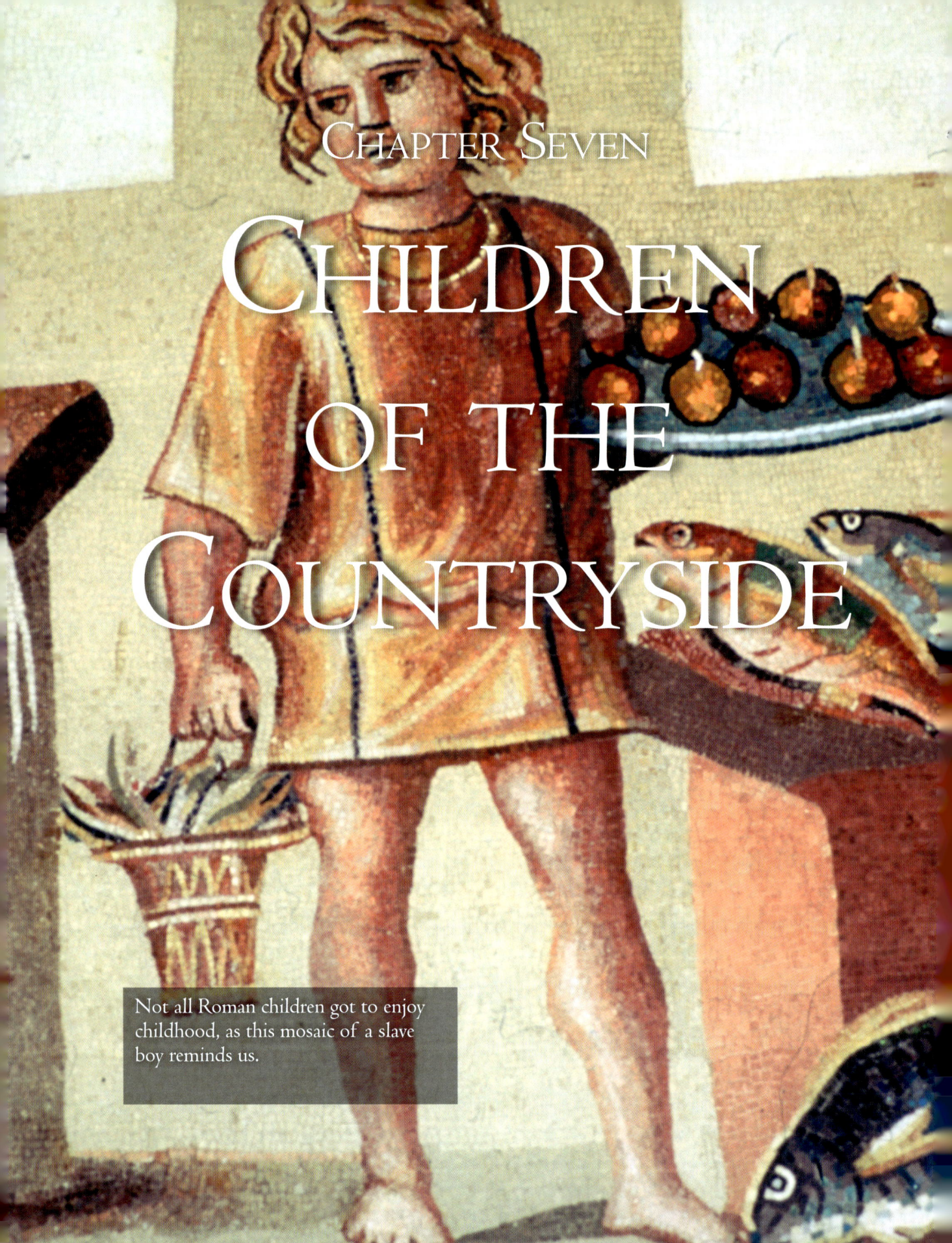

# Chapter Seven

# Children of the Countryside

Not all Roman children got to enjoy childhood, as this mosaic of a slave boy reminds us.

*"For agriculture neither pupils nor teachers have been discovered."*

*—Columella*

Though Columella felt that agriculture had to be learned through hands-on trial and error, children in Rome did receive an education—even in the country. Often students received instruction at home. Students learned to read, write, and complete basic math. Of course, education was reserved for the upper classes, and boys received more education than girls. For many children in the country, there was little time for anything but work. As children got older, they were expected to take on increasing responsibility around the farm.

## MAKING AN ENTRANCE

In the Roman Empire, nearly all babies were born at home. In the countryside, however, some hardworking women had their babies outdoors. Varro related that when he was traveling in what is now Bosnia, he saw that "pregnant women, when the time for delivery has arrived, often withdraw a short distance from where they are working, give birth there, and come back with the child you would think they had found, not borne." Afterward, these women carried their babies around with them while they worked; Varro saw women nursing their babies even while they were hauling firewood.

Some babies, unfortunately, did not receive a joyful welcome. Because there was no reliable method of family planning, parents might already have more children than they could provide for. An extra mouth to feed could be a real burden. There were very few public assistance programs for families in this position, especially in the countryside; nor were there foster-care systems or adoption agencies. Some impoverished parents felt their only option was to expose, or abandon, their newborns, leaving them outdoors to either die or be picked up by a passerby. This was a common practice throughout the ancient world.

It was the father's decision whether to raise a baby or expose it. Men were more likely to abandon daughters than sons because it was felt that girls could not contribute as much to the family, and they would require a **dowry** in order to get married. A mythological story retold by Ovid in his *Metamorphoses* was based on such a situation. In the story, a husband, Ligdus, says that he will expose his wife's baby if it is a girl. Ligdus's wife, Telethusa, *does* give birth to a girl. Telethusa passes her daughter off as a boy, saving her life.

## Growing up Fast

Upper-class children were largely cared for by slaves, often including a woman who nursed them. But most rural babies were breastfed by their own mothers, probably for about two years. A peasant mother had little assistance with childcare, unless she had an older daughter who could help out.

Soon after children were toddling, they were probably given simple chores to do. Still, while they were quite young, they did have some playtime. Most rural children were likely to have few toys. On the other hand, they would find plenty of things around the farmyard and fields to play with. A fallen branch could be a pretend sword; a large flower might make a beautiful, if not

# The Naming Ceremony

Babies were named nine days after birth in a special ceremony called the *lustratio*. According to historians in the *Handbook to Life in Ancient Rome*:

> *Lustratio* (lustration) was a purification ceremony to provide protection from evil influences and bring good luck. It consisted of a solemn procession of a beneficial object, such as an animal for sacrifice, around whatever was to be purified, with prayers and sacrifices being offered at various points on the route.

Thus, the ceremony took place in several circumstances, not just for the naming of a child. Scholars have observed that during the purification ceremony for a baby, those taking part walked in a circle around the newborn.

Names could be complex. In fact, later in the empire, it became common for Romans to go by three names instead of two. Names listed in official records included additional information like the name of a person's tribe, bringing the count up to four or five parts! Historians say that of these five parts, the equivalent to today's surname (last name) carried the most weight. Towards the end of the empire, people stopped using the four- and five-name system.

Roman diversions
included dice games.

long-lasting, doll. A poem by Tibullus mentions country children building miniature cottages out of sticks. There was also plenty of room to run around in the fresh air, and we know that children enjoyed games similar to leapfrog, tag, and blindman's buff.

Various ball games were popular, too, including ones that resembled dodgeball, soccer, and field hockey. On a farm it was easy to find materials to make a ball. Some ancient types of balls were made of wool. Others were constructed from inflated pig bladders wrapped tightly in pigskin or leather. A ball that bounced fairly well could be made from cut-up sponges with string wound around them to make a sphere, all sewn into a cloth cover.

Young people then, as now, were often high-spirited. And if they happened to be rich kids on a visit to their country estates, they sometimes were not very considerate of the hardworking locals. Young men might be particularly rowdy and likely to disrupt peasants' routines. In the following passage, Marcus Aurelius—heir to the imperial throne and future philosopher—gleefully writes to his tutor about the trouble he caused for two shepherds and their flock:

> When father was on the way home from the vineyards I jumped on my horse as I always do and set off down the road. I hadn't gone far when I saw a large flock of sheep huddled together in the road as they do in places where the way is narrow. There were four dogs and two shepherds and nothing else. Then one of the shepherds, when he spotted our little gang riding up, shouted to the other one, "See them horsemen? They're the biggest robbers out!" When I heard this I dug my spurs into my horse and galloped straight into the sheep. They scattered in panic … baa-ing and bleating. One of the shepherds hurled his crook and it struck the man riding behind me. We beat it! The shepherd who was worried about losing his sheep broke his crook!

The older a child got, the more work he or she was expected to do, whether slave or free. Girls were taught woolworking quite young. On estates, slave girls and boys looked after the sheep and goats that were kept on the farm. (Only grown men and women went with the flocks to distant pastures.) By the time they were ten or eleven, most rural children were working just as hard as the adults, and at almost as many tasks. The only things they really couldn't do yet were the jobs that took a lot of strength, such as plowing. But before many more years passed, they would be getting married and taking their full places in the adult world.

# Chapter Eight

# Trials
# and
# Triumphs

Though rural Romans enjoyed better, fresher food, there were downsides to country living.

*"Permit my harvests, my grain, my vineyards, and my plantations*
*to flourish and come to good issue."*
*—A prayer recounted by Cato*

Running a farm required a significant investment of time, energy, and of course, money. The larger the estate, the more landowners had invested. When a farm was running smoothly (and the weather cooperated), there was money to be made. Yet when obstacles arose, landowners stood to lose both wealth and status.

## HARDSHIPS

Diseases, of both people and animals, added to the burdens of rural life. Many illnesses and injuries that can easily be treated now, or even prevented in the first place, were fatal in the ancient world. There were not as many medicines available, and there was a less thorough knowledge of the workings of the human body and of surgical techniques. The possibility of crop failure also made famine a constant danger, and malnutrition was common.

A drought or other calamity could become even worse because of greed. For instance, in the late second century CE, Galen, a doctor, wrote about what happened in one area that had suffered several years of bad harvests. The people of the town went out and stripped the fields bare. Because of this, the country dwellers had nothing to eat except for what they found foraging. Nearly all the rural people developed diseases related to malnutrition, as well as conditions such as ulcers and tumors.

## JOYOUS OCCASIONS

The weekend was unknown in the Roman Empire, although its Jewish population did observe a weekly day of rest. For others, every day was a workday—unless it was a holiday. Fortunately, there were many of these. On some of them, most work was forbidden by law—but farmers might feel that they had too much to do and could not afford to rest. Virgil wrote:

> Yes, even on holy days laws human and divine
> permit some work to be done. No ordinance forbids
> to irrigate the sown field or to fence it off,
> make ready snares for birds, burn up briers and thorns.

Slaves also had to work when others were relaxing and celebrating, although we know that some slaves, at least, were guaranteed a certain number of days off a year. When farmers did get to rest and enjoy a holiday, they liked to gather together family and friends—and often the laborers, too—for eating, drinking, and dancing. Country celebrations were usually outdoors, and in the summer people might build leafy bowers to provide extra shade. There might also be competitions, such as footraces, wrestling matches, and javelin-throwing contests. Nearly all Roman holidays had a religious significance, so prayers and ceremonies played a part in the day's activities, too.

A number of Roman festivals honored the events of the agricultural year. Naturally, these were particularly beloved celebrations in the countryside. Some of the most important were the Terminalia, the Parilia, the Robigalia, and the Ambarvalia.

# Attacks at the Margins

There was one hardship that most people in the Roman Empire were safe from during the first two centuries CE. That was warfare, which in other times and places throughout history has taken a terrible toll on the countryside and its inhabitants. There were, of course, people who resented Roman rule and the military occupation of their lands, and sometimes these resentments flared up into rebellions. But most of the empire's residents seemed to agree with Tacitus when he wrote that Romans' presence ultimately brought peace.

Thanks to Rome's strength, only communities near the empire's borders really had to worry about being attacked. This is the situation described by Ovid, living in exile on the west coast of the Black Sea, less than 100 miles (160 km) from the Danube frontier:

> Countless tribes round about threaten cruel war, thinking it base to
> live if not by plunder … When least expected, the foe swarms upon us
> like birds, and when scarce well seen is already driving off the booty …
> Rare then is he who ventures to till the fields, for the wretch must
> plow with one hand, and hold arms in the other. The shepherd wears a
> helmet … and instead of a wolf the timorous ewes dread war.

Holidays afforded Roman farmers the opportunity for a much-needed break.

The Countryside in the Roman Empire

The Terminalia occurred on February 23, when neighbors gathered at their terminus, the stone or post that marked the boundary between their lands. The head of each family placed on the terminus a small cake and a garland of flowers, and they set up an altar in front of it. Then, in the words of Ovid:

> Hither the farmer's country wife brings with her own hands on a sherd the fire which she has taken from her own warm hearth. The old man chops up wood … Then he gets the kindling flames going with dry bark; his boy stands by holding the broad basket. After he has tossed corn [grain] three times into the fire his little daughter offers the pieces of honeycomb. Others hold out jars of wine; portions of each are cast into the flames. The company, dressed in white, look on in holy silence.

The Parilia

The Parilia arrived on April 21. This festival honored Pales, the goddess of shepherds. In the morning, shepherds or flock owners faced the east and repeated a prayer four times, asking the goddess to protect both people and animals. At the end of the prayers, the worshipper washed with the morning dew, then made an offering of mixed milk and wine. At the celebration's peak, sheep were driven through the smoke of a bonfire to purify them. Then, as the flames died down, shepherds took turns leaping over the fire.

On April 25 came the Robigalia, which often took place in a grove of trees. This holiday's ceremonies were designed to keep rust and mildew away from the ripening grain. Ovid even recorded a prayer to the god of rust in his poem *Fasti*.

The Ambarvalia, at the end of May, was a day of purifying the fields and crops. No one was supposed to do any work, including the oxen, who usually pulled the plow—they were left in their stalls, garlanded with flowers, and given extra hay to eat. Everyone who wanted to take part in the ceremony was required to put on clean clothes and wash their hands in running water. Then they made a silent procession around the boundaries of the fields, leading a pig, a sheep, and a bull. Later there would be a feast, with music, singing, and dancing into the night.

Life in the Roman Empire was hard, full of suffering for many and never-ending work for most. Yet there was much beauty, too, as poets and painters have shown us in their images of the countryside. Those who lived close to the land paid attention to its natural cycles and honored them with prayers and celebrations. The humblest farmer knew that a spring of pure water or a grove of trees was something special. The ancient Romans can inspire us, too, to take time now and then to remember the preciousness of nature and our rural areas, and to think gratefully of the many people who work so hard on farms around the world.

# GLOSSARY

**atrium**

The front room of a Roman house, used to receive visitors.

**bailiff**

A landowner's agent, who managed all or part of his property for him.

**barbarian**

For the Romans, barbarians were people and nations who did not speak Latin or Greek and did not share in Greco-Roman culture.

**brazier**

A pan to hold smoldering charcoal that was used as a heat source.

**dowry**

Money, goods, and/or property that a bride's family gave her to bring into her marriage.

**freeholders**

People who owned and farmed their own land; sometimes called smallholders, since such farms were usually just large enough to support a family.

**frescoes**

Wall paintings made on fresh plaster.

**inscription**

Words written on or carved into lasting materials such as metal and stone.

**javelin**

A type of spear.

**legion**

A unit of the Roman army, made up of about five thousand men.

**matron**

A freeborn married woman.

**mattock**

A digging tool similar to a pickax.

**mosaic**

A picture or design made from small square stones.

**procurator**

An official who ran an estate or mine on behalf of the emperor.

**province**

A territory of the Roman Empire.

**sharecropper**

A farmer who worked land owned by someone else.

**tenant farmer**

A farmer who rented his farm from a landowner.

**tribute**

The taxes—in particular grain and other products—that a province had to pay to the Roman government.

**villa**

A country home or estate.

**wattle and daub**

A building technique using a framework of wooden posts with flexible sticks woven between them (the wattle), filled in with a mixture of mud, clay, and straw (the daub).

# FURTHER INFORMATION

## Books

Cato, Marcus Porcius. *Cato on Farming: A Modern Translation (De Agricultura).* Translated by Andrew Dalby. Totnes, UK: Prospect, 1998.

Ermatinger, James William. *The World of Ancient Rome: A Daily Life Encyclopedia.* Santa Barbara, CA: ABC-CLIO, 2015.

Hanel, Rachael. *Ancient Rome: An Interactive History Adventure.* Mankato, MN: Capstone Press, 2010.

## Websites

**The History Guide: Lectures on Ancient and Medieval European History**

http://www.historyguide.org/ancient/ancient.html

This website provides a vast archive of lectures about the history of ancient Rome. Explore a wealth of information about life throughout the empire, including a lecture called "A Brief Social History of Ancient Rome."

**Internet Ancient History Sourcebook**

http://legacy.fordham.edu/halsall/ancient/asbook.asp

Fordham University's Internet Ancient History Sourcebook is a repository for translated texts and informational articles organized by topic. Learn about everything from life in the provinces to slaves' roles in agriculture from primary sources.

**The Roman Empire: In the First Century**

http://www.pbs.org/empires/romans

This PBS website includes a timeline, "virtual library," and even a game that lets you try your hand at running the Roman Empire.

## ORGANIZATIONS

**The Museum of Fine Arts, Boston**

Avenue of the Arts

465 Huntington Avenue

Boston, Massachusetts 02115

(617) 267-9300

Website: http://www.mfa.org

The Museum of Fine Arts, Boston features a collection called "Art of the Ancient World." Collection highlights are also catalogued online.

**The Museum of London**

150 London Wall

London EC2Y 5HN

(020) 7001-9844

Website: http://www.museumoflondon.org.uk

The Museum of London hosts a permanent collection of Roman artifacts. Their website also provides fact sheets about ancient Rome, including a biography of Boudicca.

# SOURCE NOTES

## Chapter 1: The Backbone of the Empire

p. 7, Cato, Marcus Porcius, and Marcus Terentius Varro. *On Agriculture*. Translated by William Davis Hooper and Harrison Boyd Ash. Cambridge, MA: Harvard University Press, 1935. p. 9

p. 9, Highet, Gilbert. *Poets in a Landscape*. New York: Alfred A. Knopf, 1957. p. 129

p. 9, White, K. D. *Country Life in Classical Times*. Ithaca, NY: Cornell University Press, 1977. p. 93

p. 13, Shelton, Jo-Ann. *As the Romans Did: A Source Book in Roman Social History*. 2nd ed. New York and Oxford: Oxford University Press, 1998. pp. 286–287

## Chapter 2: Rural Lifestyles

p. 15, Cato, Marcus Porcius, and Marcus Terentius Varro. *On Agriculture*. Translated by William Davis Hooper and Harrison Boyd Ash. Cambridge, MA: Harvard University Press, 1935. p. 57

p. 19, Wells, Colin. *The Roman Empire*. 2nd ed. Cambridge, MA: Harvard University Press, 1992. pp. 227–228

## Chapter 3: Country Homes

p. 23, Carlsen, Jesper. *Vilici and Roman Estate Managers Until AD 284*. Rome: L'Erma Di Bretschneider, 1995. p. 89

p. 24, Vitruvius. *The Ten Books on Architecture*. Translated by Morris Hicky Morgan. New York: Dover Publications, 1960. pp. 39–40

p. 25, Highet, Gilbert. *Poets in a Landscape*. New York: Alfred A. Knopf, 1957. p. 153

p. 30, Shelton, Jo-Ann. *As the Romans Did: A Source Book in Roman Social History*. 2nd ed. New York and Oxford: Oxford University Press, 1998. pp. 173–174

## Chapter 4: On the Farm

p. 33, Wiedemann, Thomas E. J. *Greek and Roman Slavery*. Baltimore: Johns Hopkins University Press, 1981. p. 130

p. 36, Apuleius. *The Golden Ass*. Translated by Jack Lindsay. Bloomington: Indiana University Press, 1962. p. 192

p. 41, White, K. D. *Country Life in Classical Times*. Ithaca, NY: Cornell University Press, 1977. p. 75

## Chapter 5: Rugged Men

p. 43, Cato, Marcus Porcius, and Marcus Terentius Varro. *On Agriculture*. Translated by William Davis Hooper and Harrison Boyd Ash. Cambridge, MA: Harvard University Press, 1935. p. 5

p. 44, White, K. D. *Country Life in Classical Times*. Ithaca, NY: Cornell University Press, 1977. p. 20

p. 46, Ibid., p. 61

## Chapter 6: Strong Women

p. 51, Carlsen, Jesper. *Vilici and Roman Estate Managers Until AD 284*. Rome: L'Erma Di Bretschneider, 1995. p. 122

p. 52, Shelton, Jo-Ann. *As the Romans Did: A Source Book in Roman Social History*. 2nd ed. New York and Oxford: Oxford University Press, 1998. p. 290

p. 53, White, K. D. *Country Life in Classical Times*. Ithaca, NY: Cornell University Press, 1977. pp. 75–76

p. 55, Shelton, Jo-Ann. *As the Romans Did: A Source Book in Roman Social History*. 2nd ed. New York and Oxford: Oxford University Press, 1998. p. 305

## Chapter 7: Children of the Countryside

p. 57, Carlsen, Jesper. *Vilici and Roman Estate Managers Until AD 284.* Rome: L'Erma Di Bretschneider, 1995. p. 63

p. 58, White, K. D. *Country Life in Classical Times.* Ithaca, NY: Cornell University Press, 1977. p. 76

p. 59, Adkins, Lesley, and Roy A. Adkins. *Handbook to Life in Ancient Rome.* New York and Oxford: Oxford University Press, 1994. p. 279

p. 61, White, K. D. *Country Life in Classical Times.* Ithaca, NY: Cornell University Press, 1977. p. 76

## Chapter 8: Trials and Triumphs

p. 63, Cato, Marcus Porcius, and Marcus Terentius Varro. *On Agriculture.* Translated by William Davis Hooper and Harrison Boyd Ash. Cambridge, MA: Harvard University Press, 1935. p. 123

p. 64, Lewis, Naphtali, and Meyer Reinhold, eds. *Roman Civilization, Sourcebook II: The Empire.* New York: Harper & Row, 1966. p. 108

p. 65, White, K. D. *Country Life in Classical Times.* Ithaca, NY: Cornell University Press, 1977. p. 61

p. 68, Ibid., p. 100

# BIBLIOGRAPHY

Adkins, Lesley, and Roy A. Adkins. *Handbook to Life in Ancient Rome*. New York and Oxford: Oxford University Press, 1994.

Apuleius. *The Golden Ass*. Translated by Jack Lindsay. Bloomington: Indiana University Press, 1962.

Boardman, John, et al., eds. *The Oxford Illustrated History of the Roman World*. Oxford and New York: Oxford University Press, 1988.

Cornell, Tim, and John Matthews. *The Roman World*. Alexandria, VA: Stonehenge Press, 1991.

Editors of Time-Life Books. *Rome: Echoes of Imperial Glory*. Alexandria, VA: Time-Life Books, 1994.

————. *What Life Was Like when Rome Ruled the World: The Roman Empire 100 BC–AD 200*. Alexandria, VA: Time-Life Books, 1997.

Fantham, Elaine, et al. *Women in the Classical World: Image and Text*. New York and Oxford: Oxford University Press, 1994.

Grant, Michael. *The World of Rome*. New York: Praeger Publications, 1969.

Hallett, Judith P. "Women in the Ancient Roman World." In *Women's Roles in Ancient Civilizations: A Reference Guide*, edited by Bella Vivante, 257–289. Westport, CT: Greenwood Press, 1999.

Highet, Gilbert. *Poets in a Landscape*. New York: Alfred A. Knopf, 1957.

James, Peter, and Nick Thorpe. *Ancient Inventions*. New York: Ballantine Books, 1994.

Lewis, Naphtali, and Meyer Reinhold, eds. *Roman Civilization, Sourcebook II: The Empire*. New York: Harper & Row, 1966.

Shelton, Jo-Ann. *As the Romans Did: A Source Book in Roman Social History*. 2nd ed. New York and Oxford: Oxford University Press, 1998.

Tacitus. *Dialogus, Agricola, Germania*. Latin text, with facing-page translation by Sir William Peterson. Cambridge, MA: Harvard University Press, 1914.

Vitruvius. *The Ten Books on Architecture*. Translated by Morris Hicky Morgan. New York: Dover Publications, 1960.

Wells, Colin. *The Roman Empire*. 2nd ed. Cambridge, MA: Harvard University Press, 1992.

White, K. D. *Country Life in Classical Times*. Ithaca, NY: Cornell University Press, 1977.

# INDEX

Page numbers in **boldface** are illustrations. Entries in **boldface** are glossary terms.